We All Got Our S$!t, this is Mine!

Tiffany Jones-Fisher

Presentation by *BookLeaf Publishing*

Web: www.bookleafpub.com

E-mail: info@bookleafpub.com

ISBN:9789358318852

First edition 2023

Shadows Always Follow Me

Oh, shadows, silent companions,
Ever at my side,
You dance and stretch and twist with me,
As the sun moves in the sky.

In the morning light, you're short and stout,
A dark reflection on the ground.
But as the sun climbs high, you grow long and
thin,
A silent witness to my every sound.

At noon, you disappear,
A fleeting glimpse of what I could be.
But as the sun begins to wane, you reappear,
Growing stronger with each passing degree.

In the evening light, you're long and dark,
A reminder of the day that's come and gone.
But even in the darkest night, you're there,
A silent companion, never truly gone.

Oh, shadows, what mysteries do you hold?
What secrets do you hide?
Are you a reflection of my soul,
Or a glimpse of the world beyond?

I know not, but I'm grateful for your presence,
My silent companions, my constant friends.
You remind me that I am never alone,
Even in the darkest of ends.

Pretty BIG Lies

My feelings, in the shadows you dwell,
A secret love, a hidden spell.
You long for more than just a taste,
But know your heart will go to waste.

He whispers sweet words in your ear,
Promises that you hold so dear.
But when the sun begins to rise,
He's gone, leaving you with lies.

Oh, girl, why do you stay?
Knowing that he'll never give his heart away?
Is it the thrill of the chase?
Or the hope that one day he'll change his ways?

But know this, my dear, you deserve so much
more,
Than a man who will never leave his door.
You deserve a love that's true and pure,
A love that will make your heart soar.

So let him go, and set yourself free,
Find a love that's worthy of you and me.
A love that will last a lifetime long,
A love that will never go wrong.

Oh, side chick, you're not alone,
Many before you have walked this road.
But know that there is a better way,
A love that will brighten your every day.

Jason, My Heart Still Hurts...

My dearest love, my heart's delight,
You're gone from me, both day and night.
My world is dark, my soul in pain,
I'll never be the same again.

I wake each morn, and reach for you,
But you're not there, my heart is blue.
I go about my daily task,
But all I do is think of what we had.

I see your face in every crowd,
I hear your voice in every sound.
My heart aches for you, my love so dear,
I wish you were still here.

I know that time will heal my wounds,
But I'll never forget the love we found.
You'll always be in my heart, my dearest one,
Until we meet again, when life is done.

Oh, my beloved husband, I miss you so,
But I know that you're in a better place, you
know.
You're watching over me, my guiding light,
Until we're reunited, my love so bright.

Guhh, I know YOU Tired!

Oh, single mother, you're a force to behold,
A warrior, a survivor, a heart of gold.
You wear many hats, play many roles,
But your love for your children never grows old.

You juggle work, school, and home life with
ease,
Even when you're feeling lost and unsure.
You put your children first, always and above
all,
Even when you're feeling like you're about to
fall.

You're the teacher, the nurse, the cook, and the
friend,
The one who's always there, until the very end.
You teach your children to be strong and brave,
To follow their dreams, and never be a slave.

Oh, single mother, you're an inspiration,
To us all, you're a revelation.
You show us what it means to be truly strong,
To carry on, even when things go wrong.

So thank you, single mother, for all that you do,

For your love, your strength, and your courage
so true.
May your days be filled with joy and laughter,
And may you know that you're a real superstar.

My Dearest Cameryn...

To my teenage daughter, my precious bloom,
You're the light that brightens my every room.
Your laughter is music, your heart is pure,
I'm so blessed to have you, my dear, that's for
sure.

I know that teenage years can be tough,
A time of change, both inside and out.
But know that I'm always here for you,
To support you through and through.

So fly, my daughter, spread your wings,
Explore the world, and all it brings.
But never forget your roots, your home,
And the love that I have for you, all alone.

Be true to yourself, be bold and brave,
Don't let anyone tell you what you can't achieve.
You're capable of great things, I know it's true,
So reach for the stars, and make your dreams
come true.

I love you more than words can say,
My precious daughter, my shining ray.

Remember, no matter what life throws your way,
I'll always be here for you, every single day.

It's Pepper in My Milk!

O black woman in a white world,
Your strength and beauty shine.
Your resilience is unbreakable,
Your spirit so divine.

Through trials and tribulations,
You rise above the rest.
A beacon of hope and inspiration,
You're truly blessed.

In a world that often tries to dim your light,
You shine brighter than ever.
Your voice is loud, your message clear,
You're a force to be reckoned with, my dear.

O black woman in a white world,
Know that you are worthy of love and respect.
Your presence is a gift, your essence sacred,
Your impact will forever be etched.

So hold your head high, and walk with pride,
For you are the embodiment of strength and
grace.
O black woman in a white world,
Your future is bright, your legacy will stay.

These Ducks Ain't in a Row

I'm lost, adrift in a sea of doubt,
My compass broken, my path unknown.
I wander aimlessly, searching for answers,
But all I find is darkness and gloom.

My mind is a jumbled mess,
My heart is heavy with despair.
I feel so alone and helpless,
Like a ship without a sail.

I've tried to find my way back,
But all the roads seem to lead nowhere.
I'm trapped in this labyrinth of confusion,
And I don't know how to escape.

But deep down, I know that I'm not alone.
Others have felt this way too.
And if they can find their way out,
Then so can I.

So I'll keep searching, keep wandering,
Until I find my way again.
I'll trust my instincts, and follow my heart,
And know that I'm strong enough to overcome.

For I am not lost, I am simply finding my way.

Grit & Grind

I'm tired of trying,
Tired of giving my all.
It seems like no matter what I do,
I'm always falling short.

I'm tired of being disappointed,
Tired of feeling like a failure.
I'm tired of putting my heart on the line,
Just to have it broken over and over again.

I'm tired of pretending that I'm strong,
When I'm really feeling weak.
I'm tired of hiding my tears,
When all I want to do is scream.

I'm tired of trying to please everyone,
When all it does is make me miserable.
I'm tired of putting others before myself,
When I'm the one who needs the love the most.

But I know that I can't give up.
I have to keep trying,
Even when it's hard.
Because I know that one day,
All my efforts will pay off.

So I'll keep my head held high,
And I'll keep fighting for what I want.
Even when I'm tired of trying,
I know that I have to.

Because I'm worth it.

Take Your Ass to Sleep!

In a mind where thoughts race,
A relentless, frantic pace,
Anxiety takes hold,
A chilling grip, uncontrolled.

Like a storm brewing dark,
It engulfs with its stark,
Whispers of doubt and fear,
That make the future unclear.

The heart beats fast,
As the breath is caught in a gasp,
The mind spirals down,
In a vortex that drowns.

Every little thing,
Becomes a source of sting,
Overthinking takes its toll,
As worries take control.

It's a battle within,
A constant struggle to grin,
To put on a brave face,
While inner turmoil takes its place.

But amidst the chaos,
There's a glimmer of hope,
A beacon in the night,
Guiding towards the light.

For anxiety may loom,
But it doesn't consume,
With strength and courage,
It can be managed and urged.

So take a deep breath,
And find your own path,
To soothe the anxious mind,
And peace you'll find.

For you are not alone,
In this fight you've shown,
That you have the power,
To overcome this hour.

So let not anxiety define,
The person you are inside,
For you are strong and capable,
Of living a life that's stable.

I Ain't Got Time Today

At crossroads we stand,
Where paths diverge and meander,
Decisions to be made,
Our future to meander.

The right choice, elusive it seems,
Amidst the fog of dreams,
We weigh the pros and cons,
As time relentlessly runs.

Fear whispers in our ear,
Of paths that lead to despair,
But courage bids us to stride,
Towards the unknown with pride.

We listen to our inner voice,
That guides us with its poise,
It speaks of values and goals,
Of dreams that make our soul whole.

The right decision may not be clear,
But it's the one that holds us dear,
The one that aligns with our being,
The one that sets our spirit free.

So let us not be afraid to choose,
To embrace the unknown, to lose,
For in making decisions we grow,
And on the path of self-discovery we go.

May our choices be wise,
And lead us to where our dreams lie,
May they bring us joy and fulfillment,
And a life of true contentment.

For in the end, it's not about being right,
But about living with all our might,
Making choices that make us whole,
And lead us towards our destined role.

...I Ain't Got Time Today Either!

In life's labyrinthine maze,
We face choices every day,
Decisions big and small,
That shape our rise or fall.

With every step we tread,
A path unfolds ahead,
Where options intertwine,
And consequences align.

The weight of choice we bear,
As doubts and fears ensnare,
Which path to take, which way to go,
A question that makes hearts grow low.

But amidst the tangled threads,
A guiding light ahead,
A compass within, a voice so clear,
To help us make the right choices here.

Listen to your inner guide,
Let wisdom be your stride,
Weigh your options with care,
And the right path you'll share.

Consider consequences true,
The impact on you and others too,
Let empathy be your guide,
In every step you stride.

Seek counsel when in doubt,
From those who know the route,
Their wisdom and experience blend,
To help you make decisions that transcend.

And when the choice is made,
Don't let regret invade,
Embrace the lessons learned,
As new pathways are discerned.

For every decision we make,
Is a chance for us to take,
To shape the course we steer,
And make our future clear.

So let's make choices with grace,
With wisdom and embrace,
For in the tapestry of life,
Right decisions bring less strife.

Don't Play With Me!

In a world that judges quick,
Where appearances are slick,
I stand here, unseen, unheard,
A mere speck, a fleeting word.

Labels cling, like shackles tight,
Defining me in their sight,
Less than worthy, less than grand,
Just a shadow in the sand.

Their eyes glaze over, their minds dismiss,
As if I'm nothing but a wisp,
A figment of their imagination,
A figment of their creation.

But I am here, I am alive,
With dreams and hopes that strive,
To break free from their narrow gaze,
To shine my light in their amaze.

I am not less, I am not small,
I am a being, standing tall,
With a voice that will be heard,
With a spirit that will not be blurred.

So let them stare, let them judge,
Their opinions cannot smudge,
The essence of who I am inside,
The flame that will forever guide.

I am more than what they see,
I am a mystery, a possibility,
I am a force that will not bend,
I am a soul that will transcend.

So let them view me as they may,
I will not be swayed,
I will rise above their narrow view,
And show them the me that is true.

For I am not less, I am not small,
I am a being, standing tall,
And I will not be unseen,
I will not be unheard,
I will be seen,
I will be heard.

F.O.E.

In life's chaotic dance,
Family is a steadfast stance,
A beacon in the darkest night,
Guiding us towards the light.

From the moment we take our first breath,
Family is there, till our last death,
A haven of love and support,
Where we can always resort.

They nurture us with care,
Instilling values we hold dear,
Teaching us how to love and be kind,
Helping us navigate the mind.

In times of joy, they celebrate,
In times of sorrow, they commiserate,
A constant presence, ever near,
Dispelling all fear.

Family is a tapestry woven tight,
With threads of love and pure delight,
A bond that cannot be broken,
A connection that remains unspoken.

They are the keepers of our history,
The ones who hold our identity,
The ones who know us best,
And love us without a test.

In a world that can be cold and gray,
Family is the sunshine that brightens our day,
A reminder that we are not alone,
That we belong, that we have a home.

So cherish your family, hold them dear,
For they are the ones who make life clear,
The ones who make us who we are,
The ones who shine like a guiding star.

For the importance of family cannot be denied,
It is the foundation on which our lives reside,
A gift that should never be taken for granted,
A treasure that should always be enchanted.

Don't Worry, I Got You!

In moments of strife, when burdens weigh
heavy,
A helping hand, a gesture steady,
A voice that whispers, "I'm here for you,"
Can make all the difference, it's true.

Supporting others, a noble endeavor,
Lifting spirits, helping them sever,
The chains that bind, the doubts that linger,
Guiding them towards a brighter finger.

A listening ear, a shoulder to lean on,
A presence that shows, they're not alone,
A word of encouragement, a spark of hope,
Can help them cope, and start to elope.

Supporting others is not just about giving,
It's about being there, truly living,
In their moments of need, big or small,
Standing tall, answering their call.

It's about believing in them, even when they
doubt,
Seeing their potential, helping them shout,
Their dreams and aspirations, their goals untold,

Unleashing their inner strength, bold.

Supporting others is a gift we impart,
A ripple effect, a work of art,
It spreads kindness, it builds bridges,
It makes the world a better place, it obliges.

So let us be there for one another,
In times of joy, and times of bother,
Let us be the support they need,
The ones who plant the seeds,

Of hope, of courage, of resilience,
Of dreams that come to existence,
For in supporting others, we find,
A sense of purpose, a peace of mind.

So let us be the change we wish to see,
Let us be the ones who set others free,
From the shackles of doubt, from the depths of
despair,
Let us be the ones who show them how to care.

For in supporting others, we support ourselves,
We build a community where everyone delves,
Into the depths of their potential,
And together, we make the world a more
sentimental,
A more compassionate, a more loving place,

Where everyone has a safe embrace.

Forgiving ain't Easy

In the depths of your soul,
Where shadows take their toll,
Lies a burden you carry,
A weight that makes you weary.

Mistakes made, words unsaid,
Regrets that fill your head,
A voice that whispers in your ear,
Of failures that make you fear.

But amidst the darkness, there's a light,
A glimmer of hope, ever so bright,
A chance to forgive yourself,
To set yourself free from this self-inflicted hell.

It's not easy, it's a fight,
But it's a fight worth the might,
To let go of the past,
And embrace the future that will last.

So forgive yourself, my dear,
For everyone makes mistakes, it's clear,
Learn from them, grow from them,
And move on, don't be glum.

You are not defined by your flaws,
You are more than what you saw,
You are capable of greatness,
Of kindness, of forgiveness.

So forgive yourself, and be free,
From the shackles of your own decree,
Embrace the beauty within,
And let your light shine again.

For you are worthy of love,
Of forgiveness, of a life above,
A life where you can soar,
And be the person you were meant to be,
forevermore.

Today is not Tomorrow

In fleeting moments, time does fly,
Like whispers carried by the breeze,
But amidst the chaos, there lies,
A chance to seize, a chance to please.

The gentle breeze that caresses your face,
The warmth of the sun's embrace,
The laughter that rings through the air,
The beauty that's everywhere.

In these moments, time stands still,
As joy your heart does fill,
So let go of worries, let go of strife,
And embrace the present, embrace life.

For the past is gone, the future unknown,
But the present is here, it's your own,
So cherish each moment, big or small,
And let joy within you enthrall.

Take a deep breath, and truly see,
The beauty that surrounds thee,
The flowers blooming, the birds in flight,
The wonders of day and night.

Listen to the sounds that fill the air,
The music that's everywhere,
The chirping of birds, the rustling of leaves,
The symphony of life, it weaves.

Savor the taste of food and drink,
The sweetness that makes your senses wink,
The tangy, the spicy, the sweet,
The flavors that make life complete.

Feel the warmth of a loved one's touch,
The comfort that means so much,
The embrace that makes you feel whole,
The love that fills your soul.

In these moments, find your bliss,
And let go of all that you miss,
For the present is a gift, a treasure untold,
A chance to live, a chance to unfold.

So enjoy the moment, my dear,
For it will soon disappear,
Live in the now, and let go of fear,
And embrace the beauty that is here.

Imma do Me

In depths unseen, where dreams reside,
Lies a spark, where potential hides,
A flame that burns with ardent glow,
Waiting to ignite, and let you know,

The greatness that lies within,
The power to rise and begin,
A journey of self-discovery,
Where limitations are set free.

Maximize your potential,
Unleash the force that's essential,
Break free from chains that bind,
And let your true self find.

Explore the realms of your mind,
Where hidden talents you'll find,
Embrace the unknown with zest,
And put your abilities to the test.

Don't be afraid to fail,
For in failure, lessons prevail,
Learn from mistakes, and grow from them,
And emerge stronger, like a gem.

Believe in yourself, and have faith,
In the dreams that you hold in your wraith,
For with determination and will,
You can achieve anything, and fulfill,

Your potential, vast and grand,
A masterpiece that's in your hand,
So paint your dreams upon the sky,
And let your brilliance fly.

Maximize your potential,
And make the world your testimonial,
Show the world what you're made of,
And leave a legacy that's full of love.

For you are capable of greatness,
Of achieving feats that amaze,
So don't hold back, don't be afraid,
Unleash your potential, and be amazed.

Doug

In a world that paints with hues so stark,
Where shades of black are often left in the dark,
A beacon stands, tall and proud,
My black father, a thundercloud.

His skin, a canvas of resilience,
Etched with stories of defiance,
A testament to strength untold,
In a world that often grows cold.

His eyes, pools of wisdom deep,
Where secrets and dreams sleep,
Reflecting the struggles he's faced,
And the victories he's embraced.

His voice, a rumble that commands,
Yet soothes with gentle hands,
A symphony of power and grace,
In a world that often lacks embrace.

My black father, a pillar of might,
Guiding me through darkest night,
His love, a radiant flame,
Burning bright, untamed.

In a world that tries to dim his light,
He shines ever so bright,
A beacon of hope, a symbol of pride,
My black father, in whom I confide.

So let the world see his worth,
His strength, his resilience, his mirth,
For he is a man of noble kind,
My black father, one of a kind.

Snookie

In a world that can be cold and gray,
My black mother is a radiant ray,
Her love, a warm embrace,
A safe haven, a sacred space.

Her eyes, like stars that twinkle bright,
Guiding me through darkest night,
Her smile, a beacon in the storm,
Keeping me safe from harm.

Her hands, they work with tireless might,
Nurturing me with all their light,
They wipe away my tears,
And calm my deepest fears.

Her voice, a soothing melody,
That fills my heart with glee,
Her words, they inspire and guide,
Helping me find my stride.

My black mother, she is strong,
A force that can't be wrong,
She's overcome trials and strife,
And emerged with a zest for life.

She is my hero, my guiding star,
The one who loves me from afar,
My black mother, she is my all,
The reason I stand tall.

Cameryn & Alyvia

In a world that may seem unkind,
Where shadows linger, intertwined,
Little black girls, with spirits bright,
Hold on to hope, with all your might.

Like seeds that sprout in darkest soil,
Your dreams will rise, and they will toil,
Through trials and tribulations,
They'll bloom with radiant creations.

Your skin, a canvas rich and deep,
Where beauty untold, secrets sleep,
Embrace your heritage, with pride,
Let it be your guide.

Your hair, a crown of kinks and coils,
Where wisdom whispers, and power boils,
Wear it with confidence, and flair,
Let it be your dare.

Your voice, a melody untold,
With power to inspire, and unfold,
Speak your truth, with clarity,
Let it be your legacy.

Little black girls, with dreams so grand,
The future is yours, in your hand,
Hold on to hope, let it ignite,
Your brilliance will shine, ever so bright.

So let the world see your worth,
Your strength, your resilience, your mirth,
For you are capable of greatness,
Of achieving feats that amaze us.

Little black girls, with hope in your hearts,
The world awaits your brilliant art,
So rise up, and shine your light,
And make the world a more beautiful sight.

1280 & Beyond

In a world that can be cold and gray,
Where love is often led astray,
My siblings shine with radiant glow,
Their bond, a beacon, a guiding show.

From the moment they take their first breath,
Their love for each other knows no death,
Through thick and thin, they'll always be,
A pillar of strength, for all to see.

In their eyes, a love untold,
A connection that will never grow old,
They share secrets, dreams, and fears,
Wiping away each other's tears.

Their love is a fortress, strong and grand,
A refuge from the world's harsh hand,
In each other's presence, they find solace,
A love that gives them solace.

So let the world see their love so deep,
A bond that time cannot reap,
My siblings, united as one,
A love that will forever run.

For their love is a gift, so rare and true,
A testament to the beauty of you,
My siblings, with hearts so kind,
Their love will forever bind.